HOME AND FAMILY RELATIONSHIPS

Tamra B. Orr

ROSEN
PUBLISHING®
New York

To my kids, who make sure I keep learning and changing

Published in 2010 by The Rosen Publishing Group, Inc.
29 East 21st Street, New York, NY 10010

Library of Congress Cataloging-in-Publication Data

Orr, Tamra B.
Home and family relationships / Tamra B. Orr.—1st ed.
    p. cm.—(Teens: being gay, lesbian, bisexual, or transgender)
Includes bibliographical references and index.
ISBN 978-1-4358-3579-5 (library binding)
1. Sexual minority youth—Family relationships—Juvenile literature. 2. Gay teenagers—Family relationships—Juvenile literature. 3. Sexual orientation—Juvenile literature. 4. Gender identity—Juvenile literature. I. Title.
HQ76.27.Y68O77 2010
306.760835—dc22

                                                                    2009019526

Manufactured in Malaysia

CPSIA Compliance information: Batch #TW10YA: For Further Information contact Rosen Publishing, New York, New York
at 1-800-237-9932

CONTENTS

INTRODUCTION

There are many elements that comprise who you are. One of the most important things that goes into making you a unique individual is your sexual orientation and your gender identity. Your sexual orientation determines who you are attracted to and want to form romantic relationships with. It's normal for teenagers to question their sexual orientation. Many teenagers learn that they are attracted to members of the same sex or members of both sexes. Some teenagers learn that they are transgender, meaning that their gender is different from their biological sex.

You may be questioning your sexual orientation or gender identity. Sometimes this process can seem confusing, depressing, and scary. As you struggle to figure out and accept your sexual orientation or gender identity, whatever it may be, it is not unusual to turn to the people who have been guiding and supporting you all of your life—your family. Needing your parents' comfort and advice, and wanting to talk to them about your questions and concerns, is natural. For some young people, discussing sexual orientation or gender identity with their families is fairly easy. For many, however, it isn't. The idea of discussing this with their parents or siblings might seem embarrassing or awkward. And for some teens, it can be frightening. They may worry that their parents will get angry with them, won't love them anymore, or will ask them to move out.

This book explores home and family issues that gay, lesbian, bisexual, and transgender (GLBT) teens may encounter. Coming out and living openly as a GLBT teen is a process, and it's something that you may want to take gradually. If you are a GLBT teen, you may wonder what the best strategy is for coming out to your family, understanding their reactions to the news of your sexual orientation or gender identity, and coping with feelings of sadness or rejection. You may wonder if there are organizations out there to support GLBT teens and their families. If you are a GLBT teen, there are millions of other young people just like you. They are asking the same questions, wondering the same things, and going through the same emotions that you are.

CHAPTER 1

LIVING A DAY IN THE LIFE

Many changes take place during the teenage years, and it's natural that teenagers should have countless questions in their heads. For instance, many teens have questions about fitting in, friendships, and romantic relationships. It's also natural for teens to question their sexual orientation and gender identity.

Some young people may spend endless hours mulling these questions over, changing their minds, and then starting all over again. Teens may experiment with changing how they look, who they hang out with, and who they date. There is no "correct" age by which you are supposed to have everything figured out. Things are changing so fast, it's natural that you don't have all the answers.

At some point during this discovery process, you may reach a few conclusions about who you are. Some teens discover that they are gay, while others may determine that they are,

These young people are participating in a gay pride event. It's good for GLBT teens to have a group of like-minded peers that they can talk to.

ultimately, straight. Some may learn that they are bisexual, and some may learn that they are transgender. This process of discovery is common to all teens. No matter what you may learn about yourself, remember you cannot decide what your sexual orientation or gender identity is. Sexuality isn't a choice, and it isn't something that you can change. It's simply a part of you.

Talking to a parent about your thoughts, questions, and concerns can help bring you closer together. Good communication often leads to better understanding for the entire family.

If you are at a questioning stage, you may want to talk to someone about your thoughts and feelings. Sometimes that someone is a close friend. Sometimes it's a school guidance counselor or a teacher. Many times, it is a family member, such as a sibling or your parents.

Talking to Your Parents

The answer to questions about your sexual orientation and gender identity can be rather complicated. If you are a GLBT teen, you may worry what your family might think of you if they learn that you are not hetero-sexual. Sometimes it might seem like your parents can read your thoughts, and you may worry that they'll think that something is wrong with you. You may not know what they think about people who are attracted to members of the same sex or what they think

about transgender people. You may wonder if they will accept you as a GLBT individual. You may have heard your peers make cruel jokes about GLBT people and wonder if your family also has such crude, negative opinions. You may worry that your parents will be upset or even angry with you—or that they'll simply ignore you and act like you never said anything. If you decide that it would be better not to say anything, you may wonder how long you can keep your true self a secret from your family. Maybe it would be possible to keep it a secret until you're old enough to leave home and go to college, but could you keep such an important aspect of who you are a secret for your entire life?

It's also possible that you have a family who will support you no matter what your sexual orientation or gender identity is. If you are thinking of talking to your parents about your sexual identity, begin by asking yourself some questions.

Things to Consider

Are you sure about your sexual orientation, or are you still questioning? The answer to this will influence how you approach your parents and what you do or do not say to them. How long have you been thinking about this? If this is only the first or second time that you've thought about your sexual orientation, chances are that you are still very much in the questioning stage. At this stage, it can be important to focus on being honest with yourself and asking yourself questions. You might want to take some more time to figure things out before you make any formal announcements to your family.

Are you thinking about coming out to your family because you want to? Or are you thinking about coming out because someone else thinks that you should? If coming out to your family is not your idea, you probably shouldn't do it. Coming out is a different process for everyone, and only you can determine how and when to come out to your parents. Don't come out because friends, a teacher, a therapist, or anyone else is pressuring you to. Coming out should be your decision and your decision alone.

For many young people, coming out is a tremendous relief. You are able to be honest with people and no longer have to hide who you are. Coming out should be a positive experience for you and your family. It should never be done because you are angry with your parents and want to hurt or shock them.

Your Relationship with Your Parents

How do you think your parents see GLBT people overall? Have you heard your parents make negative comments about GLBT people in the news or about GLBT characters in movies or television shows? Do you have any GLBT friends or relatives? Have you ever heard them make jokes about other people's sexual orientations? The answers to these questions can give you

High Visibility

Over the years, GLBT issues have gotten more and more media attention. Today, GLBT issues are discussed openly in politics, religion, entertainment, and many other arenas. Presidential candidates and other government officials debate the merits of same-sex marriage laws, and many states have passed legislation that recognizes same-sex marriage. Many churches accept GLBT members. The media has paid more attention to GLBT issues. There are many television shows and films that include positive GLBT characters. Because of this, GLBT issues are much more familiar concepts than they were a generation or two ago. As the GLBT community has become more public and open, acceptance of GLBT individuals has risen overall. Although homophobia and prejudice still exist, today's GLBT teens are growing up in a much more open and accepting world than their parents did.

a few clues as to how they might react to your news. Of course, remember that how they feel about some actor on television, a celebrity in the headlines, or a distant relative does not begin to compare to how they may feel about their own son or daughter.

What is your relationship with your parents like now? What has it been like for the last few years? The relationship between parents and their children can go through many changes during the teenage years. Are you close with your parents or do you argue about things very often? Have you confided in them in the past about personal matters? If so, how did they respond? Considering how your parents might react to news about your sexual orientation or gender identity can help you prepare. If they have generally reacted positively to controversial issues that are important to you or have given you the benefit of the doubt when you have something important to tell them, you might feel more relaxed when talking to them.

Sometimes parents' concern for their child's well-being can make them seem stern or disapproving. You may be surprised by how your parents react—they might be far more supportive than you ever could have dreamed. It also may take them some time to fully understand what you've told them. It's important to keep an open mind when talking to your family.

Preparation

Do you have any resources to share with your parents? Sometimes having brochures, handouts, references, books, links to the Web sites of local organizations, or other materials to share can help your parents realize that, just like you, they are not alone in this difficult process.

Have you thought about what kind of questions your parents might have for you? Take some time to do this, and try to prepare some well thought-out answers to respond with. Be prepared to explain terms and concepts that they might not be aware of. The

National Coming Out Day is an international event that has been held in October every year since 1988. Students on college campuses all over the country hold rallies for gay rights.

more knowledgeable you are, the more likely it is that they will take you seriously.

Do you know exactly what you are going to say to your parents? If not, try writing down the points you want to make. Then practice saying each one out loud until you can make your points smoothly and clearly. The more you practice actually saying things out loud, the easier they will come out. The easier they come out, the more confident you can be in saying them.

Can you show your parents what you are feeling? It may help to explain that you are feeling lonely, scared, worried, or any other emotion. By talking to them, you are showing them that you care about their feelings and that you trust them. Don't be afraid to point this out because it can help serve as a reminder to them that you may be struggling, too. Also, be prepared to give your parents the time they may need to adapt to what you have told them. Don't attempt to come out to your parents if you are not able to be patient and calm with them as they respond.

Myths and Facts

Myth: GLBT people can never become parents.

Fact: Many GLBT people are parents. Some became parents with an opposite-sex partner before they knew that they were gay. Others have become foster parents, have adopted children, or have helped raise their partner's children. Some lesbian couples opt to become parents through artificial insemination or in vitro fertilization. Some gay couples choose to become parents through a surrogate mother. There are many avenues open to GLBT couples who want to be parents.

Myth: You can always tell a person is GLBT just by looking at him or her.

Fact: There are a number of stereotypes that exist about GLBT people, and this is one of them. The truth is that there is a great deal of variation in how GLBT individuals dress, talk, and act.

Myth: Being attracted to individuals of the same sex is a personal lifestyle choice.

Fact: People cannot choose what their sexual orientation is. Just as an individual's height is not a personal preference, neither is his or her sexual orientation. People who attempt to change their sexual orientation or gender identity, whether through therapy or some other method, are invariably unable to do so.

Understanding

Turning to your parents to help you when you need guidance and support can be a wonderful thing. It can bring you closer to them. It can help them understand what is going on in your mind, and it can help you clarify your thoughts and feelings. In a best-case scenario, it will be one of those moments that you will all remember as a turning point in your lives.

Unfortunately, best-case scenarios do not always happen. It's possible that your parents might have a difficult time coming to terms with the news that you are a GLBT teen. Try to take the time to step into your parents' shoes and consider how things might seem to them. This may very well be the first time they've considered that their son or daughter might be a GLBT teen. On the other hand, you may have had months, or even years, to consider this fact.

Although it is impossible to truly pinpoint how many people in today's world are gay, bisexual, or transgender, some estimates place the number at around 5 percent of the world's population. Most people have at least one GLBT individual in their circle of family and friends. According to the 2000 U.S. Census report, there are same-sex couples living in over 99 percent of counties in the United States.

The world has changed a lot since your parents were your age. More and more states are legalizing same-sex marriage

GLBT and straight teens gather across the nation to march in parades, such as this one in San Francisco, California. Over the last forty years, the parade has gone by many names, including "Gay Freedom Day" and "International Lesbian and Gay Freedom Day Parade."

and passing antidiscrimination legislation that protects the rights of GLBT individuals. There are positive GLBT characters on television and in movies. Many school and local libraries have resources intended for GLBT students, and GLBT organizations exist all over the world. As GLBT individuals have become more visible, acceptance has followed. Although this process often seems slow, it has had a big effect.

CHAPTER 2

TALKING TO MOM AND DAD

The day has finally arrived. You've asked yourself the important questions. You are prepared to answer any questions that your family might have. You have prepared materials, practiced what you're going to say, and psyched yourself up. You are ready. Today you are coming out to your parents.

When you come out to your family, you may find that you are scared but also eager. You may be looking forward to finally revealing who you are and how you honestly feel. Today is the day.

Setting the Stage

What will the experience of coming out to your family be like? That is practically impossible to predict. No two families will react the same way. Your family may react how you expect

Selecting the right day to come out to your parents can be difficult. You should choose a day when you feel you are ready and when the timing is best for all involved.

them to, or they may surprise you. Taking time to set the stage before speaking to them can make coming out less frightening. Hopefully, both you and your family will have a positive experience.

To begin with, start by making sure you have picked a good time and place for this discussion to take place. Think about what other demands might be on your parents at any given point in the day. For example, don't talk to them as soon as they walk in the door after coming home from work. They are as eager to relax as you are at the end of the day. Don't choose a date during holidays, birthdays, or major events. Your parents might have enough on their minds already. Also, don't pick a time when they clearly have other priorities, such as getting ready to go on a trip or having company over for dinner. The night before your grandmother comes for her annual visit or before your father has a huge presentation at work may not be a good time to have a coming out discussion. If it's too late at night, they might be too tired to talk. If it's too early and they have not had their essential first cup of coffee that morning, they may be in a bad mood.

Figure out what your parents' schedules are and try to find the best time to have your discussion. Weekends are often good because there is less pressure on everyone to get up and get out of the house. Depending on what your family's schedule is, having your discussion in the middle of the day

Putting It on Paper

Sitting face-to-face with your parents and discussing your sexual orientation or gender identity may be something you want to do but you can't quite gather the nerve. Consider another option: writing them a letter. If you express yourself well through writing, this might be a good option. Putting it down on paper allows you to make sure you are phrasing things the way you want to. You can take time to express yourself without feeling rushed or pressured. If you feel shy about coming out, writing down your thoughts allows you to say what you want without anyone looking at you. You also have the time to revise and edit as you need to. It also gives your parents time to think about what you have written and decide just how they want to respond.

might be best. This way, everyone will have had a chance to wake up and there will be time to talk for as long as is necessary.

Think about a good place to have your discussion. Having it around a common gathering place, such as a kitchen table, may be a good place to start. Think about where other serious discussions have taken place before in your house. Some families might prefer an outside picnic table or a living room couch.

Wherever you choose, it should be a place where everyone can easily see and hear one another.

Before you start the discussion, also think for a moment if telling both of your parents at the same time is the wisest idea. Do you get along with one more than the other? Does one have a shorter temper? Does one understand you better? If the answer to these questions is yes, you can always break the news to one parent before the other.

Sitting Down to Talk

The moment is finally here: you are ready to talk to your family. How do you start things off? Being frank and to the point may be direct, but it may not be the best way to open up a rewarding dialogue. Your parents may have no idea that you are a GLBT teen, and the news might come as a shock to them.

It is important that you are patient with your parents and other family members. They might not react the way that you want them to. Remember that just as you have a right to every single one of your feelings, so do the members of your family. Try your best not to get angry or impatient with them. If they seem to react strangely, they may just be doing the best they can with what they know and feel at the moment. Sometimes it can be helpful to mirror the behavior that you would like to see from them. If you are hoping they will be calm, patient, compassionate, and respectful, display those

These Minnesota parents go on a walk with their son, who has recently come out as being gay. Many parents are supportive of their GLBT children.

behaviors yourself. Remember that if your mother and father react strongly, it may just mean that they truly love you and care deeply about you.

Be prepared in case your parents are totally confused by or unfamiliar with certain terms, such as bisexual, transgender, and gender identity. Be ready to define and explain each term. Don't be surprised if they feel as if you are rejecting them in some way or if they immediately begin worrying about your

Finding Help

GLBT teens are more likely than their heterosexual peers to become homeless. This is often due to their parents' reaction to their sexual orientation or gender identity. According to a 2006 report by the National Gay and Lesbian Task Force and the National Coalition for the Homeless, approximately 50 percent of all teen homelessness is caused by family conflict. They estimate that 20 to 40 percent of all homeless youth are GLBT.

Running away from home does not present a real solution to these youth, however. Living on the streets places them in a vulnerable position. They are at an increased risk for substance abuse, contracting sexually transmitted diseases (STDs), and being verbally or physically abused. It's important for GLBT teens who are not accepted by their parents or other family members to find people who support them. Friends, teachers, and GLBT organizations can all lend support to GLBT teens who are dealing with hostile family members.

safety. They may be worried that you will be the victim of a hate crime or be subjected to homophobia and prejudice. They may feel that they need to protect you from the world but don't know how. Some parents will feel very embarrassed and wonder how your sexual orientation or gender identity is going to look to family, friends, coworkers, or neighbors. Others may express relief that what they had long suspected was finally out in the open for discussion. They may feel honored that you are willing to trust them with this important information. Still, other families are going to simply reach out and tell you that they love you, regardless of your sexual orientation or gender identity.

Dealing with Negative Reactions

Although no one can say exactly how your mom or dad will react, you are not the first teen who has ever come out to his or her parents. People who work with young people and their families have identified some general reactions and questions that you can prepare yourself for. The range of responses is immense.

For instance, your parents may not believe you at first. They might think you are joking or kidding around. They might ask if are sure about being GLBT. If you are, say so. If you aren't, say that too—the teenage years are a time of transformation and discovery, and your family should understand that you might not have all the answers right away. Your parents may wonder if this is just a temporary phase you are going through.

Some parents react negatively to the news that their child is gay or transgender. Sometimes this reaction is rooted in parents' concern for their child or their ignorance of GLBT

Talking to a counselor, therapist, or other adult outside of the family can sometimes help GLBT teens communicate better with their parents and siblings. Here, students at the University of California, San Diego talk with a faculty member at the college's GLBT resource center.

issues. Other times, it may stem from overt homophobia. For some parents, same-sex sexual orientations may be against their beliefs. Parents who react this way may urge their children to see a therapist or a psychiatrist or may forbid their children from mentioning the topic of their sexual orientation in the household again. Still others might think that their child's sexual orientation or gender identity is something that can be "cured."

In extreme cases, some teens' parents burst into tears, get angry or hostile, or even threaten to throw their children out of the house. A few distraught parents might become physically or emotionally abusive. Others may be riddled with guilt, asking themselves what they "did wrong" as parents. These parents might blame one another for the fact that their child is GLBT.

These reactions are unfortunate, but they do occur. If you find that your parents react negatively when you come out, consider talking to someone in your family who is more understanding. You may also want to talk to someone outside of your family, such as a friend or school counselor. There may also be counselors in your community who are trained to work with teens.

The way parents react to the news of their child's sexual orientation and gender identity is very important. In a study published in the January 2009 issue of the journal *Pediatrics*, several university doctors took a close look at the connection between parents' reactions to being told about their GLBT teens' sexual orientation and the young adults' health risks. More than two hundred families participated in the study. The study found that the stronger the family's rejection was to the young adult's news, the higher the chances were that the teen would suffer from depression or engage in risky or self-destructive behavior. The study showed that young people whose families had severe reactions were 8.4 times more likely to report attempting suicide, 5.9 times more likely to report depression, 3.4 more times likely to use illegal drugs, and 3.4 times more likely to report engaging in unprotected sexual intercourse. In the article, Dr. Sten Vermund, physician and chair of Global Health at Vanderbilt University, states that the "study clearly shows the tremendous harm of family rejection, even if

These students at the University of California, San Diego gather in the college's GLBT resource center. Resource centers like these can help provide GLBT individuals with a sense of community.

parents think they are well-intentioned, following deeply held beliefs or even protecting their children."

Moving Forward

Although you cannot control how your parents react to the news that you are a GLBT teen, you can control how you react to them. You should have a plan and a response ready for possible reactions your parents might have.

If your family dismisses your news and does not take you seriously, your words, body language, and tone should convey to them that you are indeed not kidding around. If they ask you questions, do your best to answer them honestly but don't feel compelled to tell them more than they are asking. There is no need, especially at this point, to go into personal details. If they cry, tell them that you can see they are upset and that you are willing to answer any questions they might have. If they are confused, explain things to them in simple terms and have appropriate materials nearby to share if necessary. If they suggest you see a therapist, show that you are willing to at least briefly consider the idea, even if you don't think that you need one. If they suggest seeing a physician because you need to be treated, a gentle reminder that your sexual orientation or gender identity is not a disease requiring a cure, but rather an important aspect of who you are, might be in order. Although your parents or other family members might react strongly at first, their response could be different in an hour, a day, or a week.

CHAPTER 3

UNDERSTANDING YOUR FAMILY'S REACTIONS

While some family members may accept that you are a GLBT teen, others might have a hard time learning to accept that fact. The process by which people cope with unexpected news is different for everyone. Keep in mind that since your mother and father are different people, they will most likely react differently and exhibit their feelings in different ways. That's just part of being human.

If you have ever had something upsetting or shocking happen to you, such as a divorce in the family, an unexpected move, or the death of someone close to you, you may have found that you go through several emotional steps before finally coming to accept what happened. Author Elisabeth Kübler-Ross wrote about these stages in her landmark 1970

Not everyone is familiar with GLBT issues, but many are willing to learn. Here, a transgender individual speaks with a group of counselors about transgender issues.

book, *On Death and Dying.* Some parents experience these stages when learning that their child is not heterosexual. Everyone's path to acceptance is different, and your parents or other family members may need some time to work through their emotions. Understanding what these stages are can help you better understand your family's reaction to your sexual orientation or gender identity. They may not go through all of these stages, or they may go through them in a different order. Here are some of the steps that your parents or family might go through after you come out to them.

Denial

When confronted with the news that you are a GLBT teen, family members might experience a sense of shock. Their shock might be minor and barely noticeable. It also may be major. A parent or family member might be so shocked that he or she is speechless—or just the opposite, spewing forth emotions left and right. It all depends on your family, as well as how much they may have suspected about your sexual orientation or gender identity before you came out. Your siblings may react just as strongly—or in a completely different way. Your family's shock might soon give way to glowing acceptance.

Try your best to remember that much of what people might say during this stage primarily springs from intense

When Mom or Dad Is GLBT

According to a study done by the Child Welfare Information Gateway, between six million and fourteen million children in the United States are living with a gay parent. Colage, a national organization for children and youth with GLBT parents, provides a number of tips for GLBT parents who want to come out to their kids. When a parent comes out to his or her child, it can be an emotional time that families usually want to handle carefully and thoughtfully.

Colage's advice to GLBT parents is much the same as the advice given to GLBT teens who want to come out to their family: choose a private place, rehearse what you're going to say, take time to talk things over, and be prepared for a wide variety of responses. The organization provides resources for coming out, along with information on connecting kids in GLBT families with others as pen pals and through local chapters.

emotions, rather than logic. Back off and give your family time if they need it.

Your family may not immediately accept that you are a GLBT teen. They might believe that you are going through a phase, or they might think you are simply confused. Denying something is a way of protecting ourselves from pain and hurt.

It is a normal defense mechanism. It helps us distance ourselves from the issues we are facing, and it is completely human. For some, it comes out as fury and rage. Others experience denial as a profound sadness. Some family members might exhibit their denial by ignoring what you've told them and pretending that nothing is wrong.

Denial is a common reaction for parents to have. Your parents may have felt they knew you better than anyone else on the planet and are upset that they didn't see this coming. This experience can emphasize your independence from them, and adjusting to this can be painful for some parents.

Denial is often a brief stage. While people can deny something is happening at first, a point eventually comes when they realize that ignoring the truth doesn't make sense.

Guilt

Sometimes parents may believe that they are somehow responsible for their child's sexual orientation or gender identity. Your parents may feel a sense of guilt because they are afraid they did something wrong or made a mistake while raising you. They may wonder if they are responsible for "making" you a GLBT teen. The reasons they may come up with to explain this may seem strange or even ludicrous. Reassure them that no, they did not do anything wrong. No one is at "fault," and your

The mothers of GLBT children attend a 2003 public forum in Des Moines, Iowa. They are opposed to a proposed bill that would make it against the law for GLBT people to adopt or become foster parents in Iowa.

parents are not responsible for your sexual orientation or gender identity. Remind them that your sexual orientation or gender identity is an intrinsic part of who you are.

Grief

Many mothers and fathers believe that having a same-sex sexual orientation means their children are doomed to never get married or have children. Many also fear that their child's sexual orientation or gender identity will expose their son and daughter to homophobia or hate crimes. Your parents may be worried for your well-being and concerned how people will treat you based on who you are. They may fear that you will experience trouble and unhappiness.

This kind of concern, whether it is entirely justified or not, is just a natural part of being a parent. Even if you find it

somewhat annoying, keep in mind that it is a reaction born out of nothing but love and concern for you and your future. You can help your mother and father through this stage by talking about how being GLBT doesn't necessarily mean that you won't be able to get married some day and become a parent. Unfortunately, homophobia and discrimination are all too common in the world, but remind your parents that society is becoming more and more accepting of GLBT individuals. Also reassure them that you will not allow other people's negativity to stop you from realizing your full potential.

Acceptance

Not everyone goes through all these stages in the same order, and some people will skip an entire stage or even more than one. Your parents may immediately accept what you tell them about your sexual orientation or gender identity. They also might take weeks, or even years, to fully accept what you've told them. While you can prepare yourself to answer any questions they may have and to be patient with them, there is no way to know exactly how your family will react ahead of time. And unfortunately, there's no guarantee that they will ever reach complete acceptance.

Although it may take a long time, most families eventually will come to accept a GLBT family member. Some parents not

The organization Parents, Families and Friends of Lesbians and Gays (PFLAG) has held annual parades throughout the country since 1972.

only tolerate their son or daughter's sexual orientation or gender identity, but go on to become vocal supporters of GLBT people. They join organizations like Parents, Families and Friends of Lesbians and Gays (PFLAG), participate in discussion groups, and otherwise get involved in advocating tolerance and acceptance. If your parents do this, be sure to let them know that you appreciate it. They are telling you, in their own way, that they are proud of you and willing to support you in any decision you make. If they aren't quite ready to get involved yet, accept that as well. Given time, they may eventually choose to participate in GLBT organizations and events.

CHAPTER 4

COPING WITH DEPRESSION

After you've come out, your parents, siblings, and other family members may have completely accepted you. In fact, your relationship with them may have improved. You no longer have to pretend to be someone you aren't, and your family may be flattered that you are willing to share such important personal information with them. If this is the case, you are lucky to have such a supportive family.

Even if you have an extremely positive family, it is likely that you will still deal with some negative emotions of your own. Despite all of the advances that have been made in society's perception of GLBT individuals, the world can still be a difficult place for GLBT teens. You may find that you are struggling with anxiety, guilt, anger, or loneliness, and you may have been experiencing them for months or even years. Some of these feelings may stem from the fact that you are still questioning

These students are members of a gay-straight alliance (GSA) in Fairbanks, Alaska. They are participating in an annual event known as the National Day of Silence, which is intended to raise awareness about the bullying of GLBT students in school.

and wondering about your sexual orientation or gender identity. Or they might be the result of dealing with the fallout from the reactions from your parents, siblings, or other relatives. If you've been through a tumultuous time, it's normal to feel sad or depressed.

Hopefully these feelings will change as time passes and your family gets used to the idea of your sexual orientation or gender identity. You may also need some time to get used to accepting yourself as a GLBT teen and dealing with the challenges of living openly as a GLBT teen. How do you deal with the depression and frustration?

Depression

Everyone gets depressed or sad from time to time. Chances are that if you're feeling down, it's not because of your sexual orientation or gender identity. Rather, it's because of the stress caused by people's reaction to it. So how can you tell when depression is not just a passing mood but an actual problem that should be treated?

The answer to this question depends on who you are and what your situation is. If you are seriously depressed, you may get tired for no reason or find that you are sleeping way too much or not enough. You may feel unworthy, unhappy, or hopeless about the future. If you are seriously depressed, you

Dealing with depression can be difficult. If you start feeling so overwhelmed that you begin abusing drugs and alcohol, it's time to talk to a counselor, doctor, or someone who can listen and help.

may find that you are irritated and anxious, and you may feel too depressed to participate in the activities that you once enjoyed. You may find that you have trouble making decisions. Some people gain or lose weight when they are depressed, and unfortunately, some people turn to drugs or alcohol in an attempt to dull their feelings. Drugs and alcohol will not solve any problems, however; instead, they put the person who uses them at risk. Substance use can lead to abuse and even addiction.

In extreme cases, depression can lead people to think about committing suicide. If you find that you are considering suicide, you should talk to someone right away. The rate of depression and suicide among GLBT youth is higher than that of their non-GLBT peers. For this reason, a variety of hotlines and organizations exist to help counsel high-risk teens. It's important to understand that sexual orientation and gender identity by themselves are not risk factors for depression, substance abuse, or suicide. However, experiencing discrimination and homophobia can take a toll on GLBT teens, putting them at a higher risk for self-destructive behaviors.

Encountering Prejudice and Homophobia

The word "homophobia" refers to an irrational fear or hatred of homosexuality. People who are homophobic have no rational basis for their fear. In their prejudice, they believe that

PFLAG and other organizations are committed to helping educate people about gay and lesbian rights. They support young people and their families throughout the country.

nonheterosexual people are somehow inferior or immoral, and that hetero-sexuality is the only acceptable sexual orientation that a person can have. It's important to remember that homophobia is based in prejudice and not on facts or logic.

Homophobia can be directed at a specific individual or it can be directed at the GLBT community at large. Sometimes homophobic people display their feelings subtly and sometimes they are vocal about them. In extreme cases, very homophobic people verbally and physically harass GLBT individuals. Every year, homophobia in the United States gives rise to hundreds of hate crimes. According to the Federal Bureau of Investigation (FBI), there were 7,624 hate crime incidents

The Trevor Project

The first nationwide twenty-four-hour-a-day, seven-day-a-week suicide prevention hotline aimed at GLBT youth began with a movie. *Trevor* is a short film about a thirteen-year-old boy who tries to commit suicide after being rejected by his friends for being gay. First released in 1994, *Trevor* was aired on HBO four years later. In 1995, *Trevor* won the Academy Award for best short live-action film.

The people who made the film, writer James Lecesne, producer Randy Stone, and director/producer Peggy Rajski, suspected that some of the teens watching the film might be in the same situation as Trevor. They suggested that a helpline be broadcast at the same time as the film. To their surprise, they found that while suicide hotlines exist, there is nothing geared to GLBT teens—one of the highest risk groups for depression and suicide.

In response, they created the Trevor Project. (See the For More Information section of this book for how to contact the Trevor Project.) The Trevor Project is free and confidential, and it is staffed by volunteer counselors. The Trevor Project gets more than 18,000 calls a year and has received more than 100,000 calls since it was founded a decade ago. In addition to its support hotline, the Trevor Project offers educational kits, school workshops, online resources, and an online social networking community for young GLBT people.

committed in 2007 in the United States. Approximately 17 percent of these were based on the victim's sexual orientation.

Homophobia can extend beyond a single person's bigotry. For instance, institutional homophobia is homophobia that stems from institutions or organizations, such as governments, businesses, or religious institutions. These institutions manifest their prejudice through homophobic laws or policies. "Cultural homophobia" is the term used for an entire culture's homophobic attitude. For instance, there was a time in the United States when coming out wasn't an option for most GLBT people. Cultural attitudes were so homophobic that coming out could ruin a public figure's career and could result in people being fired from their jobs. There were no resources for GLBT teens in schools or libraries, no positive portrayals of GLBT teens in movies or on television, and no GLBT organizations to offer support to GLBT teens and adults who needed it. This has changed over the years. While homophobia certainly still exists, the world is more accepting of GLBT individuals than ever before.

It's normal to undergo a number of different emotions as you question your sexual orientation or gender identity, decide to come out to your family, and begin to live openly as a GLBT teen. Your feelings might change from day to day, or even from hour to hour. If you experience serious, prolonged depression, take time to get help. Talk to a sympathetic friend or family member, a supportive teacher, or a school counselor about how you feel.

Ten Great Questions to Ask a Teacher or School Counselor

1. **Are there any books or pamphlets I should read before coming out?**

2. **When is a good time to come out to my parents?**

3. **Should I come out to the rest of my family in person?**

4. **Where can I get GLBT educational materials to give my family?**

5. **Are there any organizations for GLBT teens and their families in this area?**

6. **How can I join or form a GLBT group, such as a gay-straight alliance?**

7. **Are there people I can talk to if I need assistance?**

8. **What should I do if my family won't accept my sexual orientation or gender identity?**

9. **How can I explain to my parents that I did not choose my sexual orientation and gender identity?**

10. **What should my parents tell family members who are having a difficult time accepting my sexual orientation or gender identity?**

Overcoming Depression

If you can't seem to shake your depression, it's possible that you should seek professional treatment. That treatment may include meeting with a therapist or seeing a psychiatrist. Remember that having to get help for your depression is not an indication of weakness. You may believe that you should just be able to "snap out of it" if you just give it enough time, but that may not necessarily be true. You may not be able to overcome depression by yourself. By seeking assistance from professionals who are trained to help GLBT teens, you are taking an active role in working to feel better. Remember that no matter what your situation is, you are still young and things will undoubtedly change for you. You still have your whole life ahead of you.

Not all depression is so serious that it can only be overcome by professional intervention. Sometimes there is much that you can do to feel better on your own. Along with possibly seeking treatment, what else can you do to combat your depression? Try to focus on doing things you enjoy, like spending time with friends, reading a good book, watching your favorite movies, or playing video games. Make sure to tell your friends that you are feeling upset or depressed; chances are they that they can help cheer you up or give you advice. Try to get enough sleep each night, as fatigue only makes depression worse. Spend time

Talking to a therapist or counselor can help you feel less alone. It gives you a safe place to express your emotions and find encouragement and acceptance.

outside in the fresh air and sunshine whenever the weather permits. Getting exercise, even if it is just talking a walk or going on a bike ride, can help as well.

It's vitally important for GLBT teens to have a supportive group of people who they can talk to. This can include friends, peers, teachers, and family members. If your family is having a difficult time accepting your sexual orientation or gender identity, having people you can turn to for help and support can make all the difference in the world.

CHAPTER 5

Finding Support

Whether you are grappling with your own feelings and questions or dealing with worried or agitated parents, or a combination of the two, it's important to get emotional support from people. You may already be close to someone, or a group of people, who can provide you with encouragement and advice. You may also want to consider reaching out to people outside of your immediate social circle.

Family Members

Even if your mom and dad are not being the most supportive people, what about other family members? Have you talked to your brothers or sisters about what you are going through? They might be able to provide wonderful, loving support for you. You might want to talk to other members of your family as

This mother voices her support of her GLBT son at a rally. Many organizations exist for the families of GLBT individuals.

well. Perhaps you have a GLBT cousin, aunt, uncle, or other relative. If so, he or she can be a wonderful person to sit down and talk to. Chances are that he or she has been through many of the same things that you're going through and can give you helpful ideas and advice. Don't forget the relatives that don't live near you, either. You might be surprised how willing they are to talk to you about what you're going through over the phone or by e-mail.

If you need to talk to a counselor, a family member can help you try to find one in your area. Professional counselors are trained to work with teens like you. If you are feeling depressed or anxious, a counselor may be able to help. In most areas, counselors must keep what you share with them confidential, which means that they can't tell anyone. Having a caring, understanding professional to talk to can be a big help.

Friends and Peers

Your friends can be one of your best sources of support. If you haven't already come out to your friends, you may want to follow the same steps you followed in coming out to your family. Prepare what you are going to say to them and be ready to answer any questions that they might have.

You may already have GLBT friends and acquaintances that you can talk to. If you don't, you can find other teens in your area by attending meetings of GLBT youth organizations. You can also

Trying to Change Yourself

Sometimes parents of GLBT teens believe that their child's sexual orientation or gender identity can be changed, despite the fact that being GLBT is not a choice or a medical condition. As of 1973, the American Psychiatric Association stopped classifying same-sex sexual orientation as a mental illness. In 2001, *The Surgeon General's Call to Action to Promote Sexual Health and Responsible Sexual Behavior* declared that homosexuality was not a "reversible lifestyle choice." The American Psychological Association officially stated, "The research on homosexuality is very clear. Homosexuality is neither mental illness nor moral depravity. It is simply the way a minority of our population expresses human love and sexuality."

Despite this, some organizations claim they can "cure" GLBT people. They sponsor camps that focus on a technique called "reparation therapy." Originally developed in the 1970s by religious groups that felt prayer was the answer for GLBT individuals, the effectiveness of these camps has never been proved. Multiple institutions believe the camps do far more harm than good. In 1990 and 1997, the American Psychological Association and the American Medical Association warned people about these camps. In many people's opinion, an individual can no more be "cured" of their sexual orientation than they can be "cured" of their height or hair color.

meet GLBT teens, as well as straight allies, by joining your school's gay-straight alliance (GSA). If you have GLBT friends with supportive parents, you might want to arrange for their parents to talk to yours. Moms and dads often relate well to other moms and dads in a way that kids can't. If you are having a hard time meeting GLBT teens near where you live, finding people to talk to online is also an option. However, be aware that meeting people online can be dangerous, and it's extremely important to protect your personal information. Don't give anyone your phone number, your address, or your real name.

School

Many schools have groups established for GLBT students. The most visible of these are gay-straight alliances (GSAs). There

Many students enjoy the friendships they make through groups like gay-straight alliances. Straight teens often join so that they can support their gay friends. Some clubs perform community service projects and fund-raisers.

are currently more than 4,400 GSAs in operation. GSAs help make schools safer for GLBT students, promote tolerance and understanding, and work to educate the school and community about GLBT issues. If your school doesn't have a GSA or similar organization, you might check with other area high schools and local colleges and universities to see what resources they might have to offer. You might also want to consider starting a GSA or similar group in your own school.

If you are considering starting your own GSA, you should ask your school's administration about its policies and procedures regarding extracurricular student clubs. If your school allows extracurricular clubs, they can't deny your request to start a GSA. GLBT clubs such as GSAs are protected under the Equal Access Act, which was passed by Congress in 1984 to protect student groups like GSAs.

You should ask a teacher or member of the school staff to be your faculty adviser. You may want to ask a school counselor for advice as to which teachers would be interested in doing this. Choose a time and place for your first meeting. Be sure to publicize your meeting by telling teachers, students, and school guidance counselors. Make posters announcing the meeting and inform your school newspaper. Write an outline of what you want to accomplish at the first meeting. On the agenda, include some fun ice-breaking activities to help people get to know each other if they don't already.

When you hold your first meeting, ask people what they are looking for in the group. Determine what the group's goals are and strategies that can be used to accomplish them in the future. Don't be discouraged if only a few people show up at first. It takes a while for groups to grow and develop. Stick with it. As your group becomes more visible, new members will be encouraged to join. Remember that some of your peers may initially be shy about joining a GLBT group, especially if they have not come out to their classmates.

Also, check for GLBT resources in your school library. Even if the library doesn't have copies of the books, videos, or other materials you are searching for, you can often obtain these materials through an interlibrary loan. All you have to do is ask your school librarian. If your school doesn't have any resources for GLBT students, you may want to talk to your school librarian or a school staff member about getting some.

Family Groups

Along with starting your own support group for your needs, you might also encourage your parents (if they are open to the idea) to join or start their own group as well. Organizations such as Parents, Families and Friends of Lesbians and Gays (PFLAG) provide support for friends and family members of GLBT individuals. Currently, PFLAG has more than 200,000

When families support their GLBT members, it sends a powerful message.

members. By joining an organization such as PFLAG, those with GLBT family members can meet a community of people just like them.

If your parents or family members are interested in starting a chapter of a GLBT organization such as PFLAG, or perhaps even starting their own GLBT community group, they should decide what kind of group they want it to be. They should also determine what kind of resources they need and what resources are available to them in the community. They also need to determine where they will hold meetings and how they will publicize their events.

Your Religious Community

Different religions have different official viewpoints on sexual orientation and gender identity. Many GLBT individuals have strong religious beliefs and remain active in their religious community after coming out. Although some faiths are adamantly opposed to any sexual orientation other than heterosexual, many of them are becoming more accepting of GLBT individuals. Some faiths even welcome GLBT clergy and perform same-sex marriages. Many have special support groups aimed at GLBT members. For some people, discussing their sexual orientation or gender identity with others of the same faith can be a great help.

This woman holds a sign supporting her son at Worldwide Pride, a gay pride event in Colorado Springs, Colorado.

The Necessity of Support

Every person's understanding of his or her sexual orientation or gender identity is unique. No two people walk the exact same path, but they may have several things in common. One of them is the need for emotional support. Having other people who understand what you are feeling and experiencing and people who love you and are willing to listen are essential. A community of like-minded people can be a great help to any GLBT teen. Families can be wonderful support groups for GLBT teens, and if you are lucky enough to have a family that helps and supports you, you may also find that you are helping support them as well. No matter what you eventually learn about who you are, being open with your family can make all the difference in the world.

GLOSSARY

artificial insemination The laboratory process of sperm being introduced into a woman's uterus for purposes of conception.

biological sex The physical sex a person is born with.

bisexual A person who is attracted emotionally and sexually to members of the same sex as well as members of the opposite sex.

coming out The process of revealing one's sexual orientation or gender identity to others.

gay A term that refers to men who are attracted to other men; it can also refer to anyone who is attracted to members of the same sex.

gender A person's gender defines whether he or she is male or female; it is a combination of physical and behavioral traits.

gender identity The gender a person identifies with, regardless of his or her biological sex.

heterosexual A person who is attracted emotionally and sexually to members of the opposite sex.

homophobia An irrational fear or hatred of GLBT people; a prejudice that has no basis in fact.

homosexuality Sexual and emotional attraction to members of the same sex.

in vitro fertilization The process by which egg cells are
fertilized outside of the mother's womb.

lesbian A woman who is attracted to other women.

prejudice Negative preconceived thoughts, feelings, or ideas
that people hold against others based on their gender,
sexual orientation, race, nationality, and other characteristics.

reparation therapy A set of methods designed to "cure"
gay individuals of their sexual orientation.

sexually transmitted disease Any disease that is passed
from one person to another through sexual contact.

stereotype An oversimplified generalization made against
a group of people; stereotypes are harmful and generally
rooted in prejudice.

straight A slang term for a heterosexual person.

surrogate A person who stands in for or performs a process
for another person. A surrogate mother becomes pregnant
with another person's child and carries it to term.

transgender A transgender person is an individual whose
gender does not match the sex he or she was born as.

Advocates for Youth

2000 M Street NW, Suite 750

Washington, DC 20036

(202) 419-3420

Web site: http://www.advocatesforyouth.org/glbtq.htm

Advocates for Youth is an organization that focuses on providing young people with information and services regarding sexual health.

Canadian Rainbow Health Coalition

P.O. Box 3043

Saskatoon, SK S7K 3S9

Canada

(800) 955-5129

Web site: http://www.rainbowhealth.ca

This organization addresses health and wellness issues specific to GLBT individuals.

Colage

1550 Bryant Street, Suite 830

San Francisco, CA 94013

(415) 861-5437

Web site: http://www.colage.org
Colage works to support individuals with GLBT parents.

Family Pride

P.O. Box 65327

Washington, DC 20035

(202) 331-5015

Web site: http://www.familyequality.org
Family Pride is a nonprofit organization dedicated to organizing and supporting both formal and informal groups of GLBT parents, youth, and families.

Gay and Lesbian Alliance Against
   Defamation (GLAAD)

5455 Wilshire Boulevard, #1500

Los Angeles, CA 90036

(323) 933-2240

Web site: http://www.glaad.org
GLAAD is dedicated to promoting fair and responsible portrayals of GLBT people in the media.

Gay, Lesbian and Straight Education
   Network (GLSEN)

90 Broad Street, 2nd floor

New York, NY 10004

(212) 727-0135

Web site: http://www.glsen.org
This organization works to support GLBT students and ensure that they
have safe school environments.

Parents, Families and Friends of Lesbians and Gays (PFLAG)

1726 M Street NW, Suite 400

Washington, DC 20036

(202) 467-8180

Web site: http://www.pflag.org
PFLAG is an organization for GLBT individuals, their families, and their
friends.

PFLAG Canada

1633 Mountain Road

Box 29211

Moncton, NB E1G 4R3

Canada

(888) 530-6777

Web site: http://www.pflagcanada.ca
PFLAG Canada works to promote the health, well-being, and happiness of
GLBT people and their family members.

The Trevor Project

9056 Santa Monica Boulevard, Suite 208

West Hollywood, CA 90069

(310) 271-8845

(866) 488-7386

Web site: http://www.thetrevorproject.org

The Trevor Project provides a twenty-four-hour-a-day crisis hotline for GLBT teens.

Web Sites

Due to the changing nature of Internet links, Rosen Publishing has developed an online list of Web sites related to the subject of this book. This site is updated regularly. Please use this link to access the list:

http://www.rosenlinks.com/glbt/home

For Further READING

Abrahams, George, and Sheila Ahlbrand. *Boy v. Girl? How Gender Shapes Who We Are, What We Want, and How We Get Along.* Minneapolis, MN: Free Spirit Publishing, 2002.

Andryszewski, Tricia. *Same-Sex Marriage: Moral Wrong or Civil Right?* Breckenridge, CO: Twenty-First Century Books, 2007.

Beam, Cris. *Transparent: Love, Family, and Living the T with Transgender Teenagers.* Orlando, FL: Harcourt, 2007.

Garden, Nancy. *Hear Us Out! Lesbian and Gay Stories of Struggle, Progress, and Hope, 1950 to the Present.* New York, NY: Farrar, Straus and Giroux, 2007.

Gillespie, Peggy, ed. *Love Makes a Family: Portraits of Lesbian, Gay, Bisexual, and Transgender Parents and their Families.* Amherst, MA: University of Massachusetts Press, 1999.

Huegel, Kelly. *GLBTQ: The Survival Guide for Queer and Questioning Teens.* Minneapolis, MN: Free Spirit Publishing, 2003.

Keen, Lisa. *Out Law: What LGBT Youth Should Know About Their Legal Rights.* Boston, MA: Beacon Press, 2007.

Levithan, David. *Boy Meets Boy.* New York, NY: Alfred A. Knopf, 2003.

Levithan, David. *The Full Spectrum: A New Generation of Writing About Gay, Lesbian, Bisexual, Transgender, Questioning, and Other Identities.* New York, NY: Alfred A. Knopf, 2006.

Marcus, Eric. *What If Someone I Know Is Gay? Answers to Questions About What It Means to Be Gay and Lesbian.* New York, NY: Simon Pulse/Simon and Schuster Books, 2007.

Peters, Julie Anne. *Keeping You a Secret.* New York, NY: Little, Brown, 2003.

Plum-Ucci, Carol. *What Happened to Lani Garver?* San Diego, CA: Harcourt, 2002.

Snow, Judith. *How It Feels to Have a Gay or Lesbian Parent: A Book by Kids for Kids of All Ages.* New York, NY: Harrington Park Press, 2004.

BIBLIOGRAPHY

Beam, Cris. *Transparent: Love, Family, and Living the T with Transgender Teenagers.* Orlando, FL: Harcourt, 2007.

Bigner, Jerry J., ed. *An Introduction to GLBT Family Studies.* New York, NY: Haworth Press, 2006.

Eduactiv.info. "My Child Is Homosexual. What Should I Do About This?" Retrieved March 2009 (http://www.educativ.info/teen/homo_sexual.html).

Federal Bureau of Investigation. "Hate Crime Statistics 2007." Retrieved March 2009 (http://www.fbi.gov/ucr/hc2007/incidents.htm).

Friedrichs, Ellen. "Is Teen Suicide a Bigger Risk If You Are GLBT?" About.com. Retrieved March 2009 (http://gayteens.about.com/od/sexuality/f/suicide.htm).

GLSEN. "The GLSEN Jump-Start Guide: Building and Activating Your GSA or Similar Student Club." GLSEN.org. Retrieved March 2009 (http://www.glsen.org/binary-data/GLSEN_ATTACHMENTS/file/000/000/974-1.pdf).

Hayhurst, Chris. "Help and Hope for LGBT Teens." Teenwire.com, February 4, 2005. Retrieved February 2009 (http://www.teenwire.com/infocus/2005/if-20050204p093-trevor.php).

Huegel, Kelly. *GLBTQ: The Survival Guide for Queer and Questioning Teens.* Minneapolis, MN: Free Spirit Publishing, 2003.

King County Public Health. "Depression and Mental Health Among GLBT People." October 7, 2008. Retrieved March 2009 (http://www.kingcounty.gov/healthServices/health/personal/glbt/depression.aspx).

Paige, R. U. "Proceedings of the American Psychological Association, Incorporated, for the Legislative Year 2004. Minutes of the Meeting of the Council of Representatives July 28–30, 2004." American Psychological Association. Retrieved March 2009 (http://www.apa.org/governance).

Safe Schools Coalition. "How Many of Us Are There?" SafeSchoolsCoalition.org. Retrieved March 2009 (http://www.safeschoolscoalition.org/HowManyOfUsAreThere.pdf).

Schneider, Ruth. "GLBT Youth at Greater Risk for Depression, Suicide Attempts." Olympian.com, January 3, 2009. Retrieved March 2009 (http://www.theolympian.com/outspoken/story/713527.html).

INDEX

About the Author

Tamra B. Orr is the author of more than two hundred nonfiction books for young adults. She has a degree in secondary education and English from Ball State University. Her book about eating disorders, *When the Mirror Lies*, won the Voice of Youth Advocates Honorable Mention Award for 2008. Her book *School Violence: Halls of Hope, Halls of Fear* won the 2006 New York City Public Library Best Nonfiction Book for Teens Award. Orr lives in the Pacific Northwest with her family.

Photo Credits

Cover Queerstock.com; cover (inset) p. 7 Shutterstock.com; pp. 8–9 Anne-Marie Weber/Taxi/Getty Images; pp. 14–15 © Bob Daemmrich/ The Image Works; pp. 18–19, 25, 34, 38–39, 60–61, 64 © AP Images; p. 21 © www.istockphoto.com/Damir Cudic; pp. 28–29, 31 © John Gastaldo/ The San Diego Union-Tribune/ZUMA Press; p. 41 © Lee Snider/The Image Works; p. 44 © Eric Engman/Fairbanks Daily News-Miner/ZUMA Press; p. 46 © www.istockphoto.com/Michael Krinke; pp. 48–49 © Dennis MacDonald/PhotoEdit; pp. 54–55 © Angela Hampton/Bubbles Photolibrary/ Alamy; p. 57 © Homer Sykes Archive/Alamy; p. 66 © Sean Cayton/The Image Works.

Designer: Les Kanturek; Photo Researcher: Amy Feinberg